BABY
ANIMALS

Maurice Burton

TREASURE
PRESS

CONTENTS

Like most carnivorous animals, lion cubs
practise on each other, in play, the kills they will
need for survival when they are mature. The
two on the left are pausing between bouts of
activity.

INTRODUCTION

A baby is strictly speaking a young or infant human-being in arms, before it can walk. In the late nineteenth century, the word began to be used fairly commonly for young animals, although only a few carry their young in their arms. Only within the last twenty or thirty years has the word been applied universally to young animals, and then solely to the very young of vertebrates, or backboned animals. The early stages of invertebrates, or animals without backbones, have always been referred to as larvae or, in some insects, as nymphs.

The new use of 'baby' to include the young of vertebrate animals as well as humans, coincides with the sudden popular and widespread interest in animals in general, that is so marked a feature of the twentieth century, at least in affluent countries. It is interesting that the love of and interest in animals generally have been particularly marked by a fondness for young animals. They appeal to us. We have an impulse to hold them, to fondle them, even to possess them. They hold our attention; and even this is of interest, and demands an explanation.

Even if in primitive or backward societies animals appeal more as objects to be hunted and as food, the baby animal still reaches out to the heart. Had this not been so, it is unlikely that animals would have been domesticated as early as they were. If we could but know, it is highly likely that the nursing and nurturing of their babies was a first step in the domestication of dogs and cats, and possibly of other animals too. This can only be speculation, and must be based on the readiness with which even primitive peoples today will foster a baby animal found in the wild. We also know how readily more advanced peoples will get a baby animal – for example, a puppy – then abandon it when it is fully grown.

In 1943, the famous investigator of animal behavior, Konrad Lorenz, analysed the phenomenon. He suggested that the parental instinct is related to the instinct to reproduce, which is a response to certain sign stimuli. He found that there are three such signs: a short face in relation to a large forehead, protruding cheeks and maladjusted limb movements. In more homely terms, Lorenz was suggesting that a baby appeals to us by its small rounded face and its general helplessness.

There is much value in Lorenz' theory. He pointed out that dolls are made to meet these three requirements. The film industry cashes in on this appeal with its use of juvenile stars – probably the most famous being the young Shirley Temple, child-star of the 1930s. The third example Lorenz gave was that childless women tend to choose pets as substitutes for babies.

This points to one weakness in the theory. For example, the dachshund tends to be a favorite pet, but cannot by any stretch of the imagination be said to have a short face. Then again, Lorenz' theory ignores other special features in the baby: voice, the lack of aggressiveness in the face and demeanor, and the large eyes in proportion to the size of the face.

There is a deeper factor, which can be summed up by the law of the sea: 'women and children first'. This is traditionally the first consideration when a ship at sea is in danger of sinking. It also operates on land and in all situations where life and limb are threatened. One example is seen in the scare in Harrisburg, Pennsylvania in 1979, when there was a suspected leak of radioactive material due to overheating in a nuclear power station. The initial step in evacuating the civilian population from the danger area was to take children and

The baby ostrich of East Africa (*right*) has strong legs for running from danger. Its prickly-looking plumage resembles a desert plant when the chick gives up running and decides to seek safety by remaining crouched on the ground.

pregnant women to a place which offered safety. What we are seeing in the matter of shipwrecks and of leaking nuclear-cores is the operation of a far wider natural law. This newly publicized biological theory states that an individual seeks instinctively to perpetuate his or her genes. King Solomon demonstrated this when he ordered a baby in dispute to be cut in two. It was the real mother who begged for its life to be spared, although the sham mother must have been equally influenced by the baby's short face, rounded cheeks and maladjusted limb movements.

Men are frequently held to have an innate chivalry towards women. If so, this may spring from a tendency to protect the bearer of his children, who carry his genes, and who thereby perpetuates his stock and, in the long run, his species. Similarly, in all situations, first consideration is normally given to a woman carrying a baby.

Human beings are no more advanced than

monkeys in this respect. Male monkeys normally do not attack the females. More especially, no normal male monkey will do bodily harm to a female of his troop who is carrying an infant. Instances have been observed where a male has threatened to attack a female, until she turns so that he can see in her arms the infant previously hidden from his view.

These observations give the background against which an answer can be suggested to the question: why do baby animals attract us? For they can be, without doubt, extremely attractive, as everyday experience shows, especially when in the form of pictures.

Perhaps it is a mistake to analyse scientifically something that is pleasing to the senses. It is like destroying a beautiful flower in order to find out and name the chemicals responsible for its color.

Yet there is something very satisfying in being able to enjoy the aesthetic or sentimental side of life while at the same time exploring how life works.

Maybe this is the difference between a picture gallery and an illustrated book; in the former it is mainly the eye that is brought into operation, whereas in a book all our mental processes are made to work. We can feast the eye on the pictures and we can feed our insatiable curiosity with the text.

At least there is a highly practical purpose served in the way adults find young animals attractive. It makes them protect the babies during the most vulnerable period of their lives. Without this, the higher forms of animal life would probably never have become established.

The sleeping chimpanzee (*above*) appears to smile as he dreams, and is oblivious of the camera. A baby roe-deer (*left*), often known as a fawn, is correctly named a 'kid'.

PETS

The keeping of pets, so universal today and undoubtedly going back to the time of primitive man, probably stems from the attractiveness of baby animals. The appealing looks of these Irish Setter puppies are a good example of the endearing qualities of the young in general. Newborn puppies are blind, naked and helpless. Later, they begin to gain independence and become playful. Their charm is then coupled with great vivacity and vigour.

Donkeys

Donkeys have always had a checkered career at the hands of their masters. At different times and in different places they have been either despised or revered. These animals are currently enjoying a resurgence of popularity which seldom can have been excelled. They are finding good homes in cities and in the countryside, or are being used as foundation stock by newly formed donkey studs.

The reason for this may be that donkeys have a pathetic expression on their faces, due almost entirely to their heavy brows which give them a perpetual downcast look. This is even more pronounced in the foal, as can be seen particularly well in the photograph above.

Small Pets

An outstanding example of *precocial* young is found in the guinea pig (*above*). Its young are born fully sighted, with a good, warm coat, and able to run about almost as soon as the mother has licked them clean of the birth fluids and membranes.

This is in strong contrast with most other rodents, such as the greater Egyptian gerbil. A family of the mother and her litter are shown here on the left. Gerbils have only recently been accepted as pets.

A better known example of a pet with *altricial* or dependent young is the European rabbit (*right*). Baby rabbits are very soft to touch, and are delightfully tame.

Kittens

Equal with the dog in the league table of favorite pets is the cat. Perhaps the most remarkable feature of the cat is that its wild relations are almost untameable, even when the kittens are taken from the mother before their eyes are open and hand-reared. This perhaps does more than anything else to explain the essential character of cats: independence. They may be tame but they are never servile.

Another outstanding feature of the cat is its deceptive appearance. Seemingly sleepy-eyed and thoroughly relaxed, it can turn to a ball of fury in a trice.

The farmyard cat, traditionally, is on the borderline between being tame and being wild. A female will accept human contact, but will retain her independence to the point of hunting for most of her food. She will give birth to her kittens in the bush and even these kittens, alluring to the eye, will bare their teeth and spit in a babyish way if approached by a stranger.

FARMYARD ANIMALS

Most farm animals were domesticated so long ago that we shall never be certain precisely how they came to be put into bondage. The animals here, for example, are a long way from their natural habitat, which was almost certainly on the undulating mountainsides of western Asia. The sheep was domesticated probably about 8000 years ago.

Newborn lambs (*previous page*) are among the most appealing of all young animals, especially in their joyous gambolling. This, like the play of any young animal, is the result of an excess of energy. The lamb receives its nourishment from its mother, and even when weaned it does not have to look far for its food, because, being a grazer, it is surrounded by an ever-present supply.

The skipping of a young lamb, although apparently purposeless, is a period of probation for the more serious side of life. It is a period of

education in the use of its muscles and of their control and co-ordination, as well as in the training of the senses.

There have been several recorded instances of a man on a bicycle being followed by the baby of some hoofed animal, for example a young antelope. This following response, as it is called, may have led to the domestication of animals. The first subjugations may well have been the result of 'catching them young'. The adults of wild cattle were called aurochs. They were huge and formidable beasts with powerful horns. To have captured such a beast alive would have presented great difficulties, and so it must have been their young that became the stock that started the several breeds of domesticated cattle that were already known in 2500 BC. On the left is the face of the young calf, a familiar descendant of those cattle.

The adult wild goat would have presented similar problems for its captors, especially during the New Stone Age, 9000 years ago, when the goat was first domesticated. Much the same can be said of the pig whose ancestor was the fierce, irascible wild boar. The tame and attractive young of the modern, domesticated species are seen in the kid on the right and the piglet below.

Foals

There is some evidence that man's first interest in the horse was in killing it for food. By 2000 BC at the latest, however, the horse had been domesticated as a beast of burden. How this was accomplished is uncertain. What we do know is that the following response is strong in foals, whether of domesticated or semi-wild parents. At the same time, a foal shows little aggression towards a would-be captor, and therefore could be readily taken alive. From birth a foal has to keep up with its mother, even when she is running. For this to be possible the foal's legs are disproportionately long, which gives it a gangling look that is so awkward and at the same time so attractive.

Farmyard birds

Ducklings (*top left*) and chicks (*bottom left*) are the young of farmyard poultry. This is the collective name for those tame birds reared for their flesh, eggs and feathers.

All poultry have precocial young, able not only to move about on their own feet as soon as they are hatched, but also able to feed themselves from the start. Unlike altricial birds, (which spend their first days in a nest, naked and blind, fed and kept warm by their parents) they have eyes fully open and are covered at first with a plumage of incomplete feathers, usually referred to as down. Cygnets (*below*), the young of the mute swan, remind us that swans were formerly poultry, tended by the swanherd.

WILD
ANIMALS

The attractiveness of baby animals is not confined to the young of pets and farm animals. In fact, it seems to be heightened in some of the wild species. For example, the adult fox behaves in a way which causes the farmer to shoot it on sight. The cub, in contrast, is singularly attractive. Newly emerged from its earth, it is chocolate-coloured and no more than a fat, furry ball on short legs, with large blue eyes.

The young red squirrel (*far right*) and the young badger (*right*) represent two wild species with utterly dependent young. In both, the babies are born blind, naked or nearly so, and helpless; but both soon become active and confident in movement, well before they are weaned. The red squirrel is a tree-dweller, and the baby must be able to cling to branches and balance itself early, in preparation for the moment when it must leave the nest, or drey, high up in the trees. The baby badger must soon learn to clamber up the tunnel from the nest in the bowels of the earth, known as the set or sett, in preparation for leaving home to forage for itself.

The baby hare, or leveret (*below*) is precocial, born with eyes open, fully-furred and able to run actively within days. It is deposited by the mother in a 'form', in a tussock of grass, where it is completely hidden.

These four young animals typify the hunters and the hunted, and illustrate the requirements in the babies of both classes of wild animals.

The baby racoon (*below*), the young coyote (*top right*) and jackals (*below right*) are all born blind, naked and helpless, and are tended and protected by their parents. All are future hunters, and are very playful, which seems to be common to babies destined to fill that role. In play, they develop the muscles and educate the senses in anticipation of the speed and dexterity needed for the seeking out and running down of prey.

Racoons are born in litters of up to six cubs. They are very small at birth and do not come out into the open until they are seven weeks old. At first they make only short journeys outside the nest, and do not start to hunt for food until seven weeks later. Racoons stay with their mothers for a year. The fathers do not help to rear the families. During the year spent with the mother racoons, the cubs learn the many different methods of hunting which they will need to use as adults. They have to learn where and when to find each kind of food.

The piglets of the wild boar (*below*), a prey animal, can get onto their feet shortly after birth, and can soon keep pace with their mother. They are born with their eyes open, and with a coat of baby bristles. This coat, unlike that of the parents, is striped. The stripes break up the outlines of the body, camouflaging it and giving it a measure of security that offsets the young animals' vulnerability.

Deer and llama

The roe-deer of Europe (*right*) and the llamas
of South America (*above*) offer an interesting
contrast in baby needs. The kid of the roe-deer,
often spoken of as a fawn but more correctly
called a kid, has a spotted coat that blends well
with the sun-dappled undergrowth in which it
is born. It instinctively lies still when danger is
near, and is hard to see against the background
of leaf-litter on which it rests. Its mother returns
to it periodically to nurse it.

The llama baby (*above*) and the baby guanaco
(*top right*), the wild ancestor of the llama, are
both born into the arid, treeless countryside of
the mountainous spine of South America. There,
speed of movement is more valuable for safety
than camouflage. So the baby, which can walk
and run soon after birth, has the gangling long-
legged build enabling it to keep up with its
mother as she wanders far in search of pasture.
The mother suckles its calf for only four months.
Both are ready to take off at speed at the first
sign of danger. The llama was first tamed by the
Incas 4500 years ago.

The one-humped or Arabian camel (*above*) probably originated from central Asia but became extinct as a wild animal too long ago for this to be agreed beyond doubt. A desert animal, its baby relies more on speed than on camouflage, like the llamas of South America (see page 30–31). The baby camel is born with eyes open, fully coated with a soft wool, and able to keep up with its mother soon after birth.

The chimpanzee (*right*), in common with other primates (monkeys and apes), is born with eyes open and body protected with a coat of long hair, characteristics typical of independent young. It is not, however, a true precocial, for its legs do not develop full strength for a while. But it is strong in the arms and able to cling to the mother's fur. The mother also clasps it to her body when she is moving about and cradles it to her when at rest.

Africa is the home of herds of large hoofed animals, the so-called 'big game' that afforded a paradise for white hunters. The white hunter apart, the continent demonstrates more strikingly than elsewhere in the world the constant war between vegetarian hoofed animals, supported by abundant vegetation and the prowling carnivores. The hoofed vegetarians rely on speed for survival and their babies consequently are precocial and long-legged, as typified by the young zebra (*top left*), baby giraffe (*below*) and the gemsbuck (*below left*).

The adult gemsbuck uses its horns with deadly effect against dogs, and even lions have been found dead after being gored by them. It is not surprising therefore that these valuable weapons are developed very early in the baby gemsbuck. The zebra foal must be active from its birth. The mare takes about seven minutes to deliver her foal. Within a short time the foal is standing up, long-legged but short-bodied. Sometimes the foal is left alone and defenseless in dry weather while the mother searches for water. But if the mother remains thirsty, she cannot feed the foal.

Bears

In the medieval natural history books, the she-bear is portrayed licking several oval objects. These are supposed to be her cubs and she is 'licking them into shape'. This fanciful idea reminds us that bear cubs at birth are extremely small and look like shapeless masses of flesh. It is not surprising therefore that bear cubs stay a long time with the mother, even after she has led them from the den in which they were born and where the early nursing takes place.

A polar bear cub's eyes do not open until the thirty-third day after birth, its ears open on the

twenty-sixth day, but its hearing is imperfect until the sixty-eighth day (*below left*). Moreover, it may not start to walk until it is nearly seven weeks old.

The brown bears are similarly slow in their development, including the family of Alaskan brown bears (*right*) and the four Syrian brown bear cubs in the Nuremburg Zoo (*below*). The number of cubs in a brown bear's litter depends on the age of the mother. A young bear will carry a single cub, but more mature she-bears will have two or three cubs. The cubs will not follow their mother into the open until two or three months after birth. By this stage they are ready to vary their diet with such things as roots, small animals and bulbs. Bear cubs are particularly playful and nimble. They climb trees, a rare adult activity, and play games.

Carnivores

The tiger cub (*below left*) belongs to the largest species of the cat family. The usual litter is three or four cubs but may be up to seven. The young are striped and blind at birth, and a cub weighs only 2–3 pounds when born. Although tiger cubs are weaned at six weeks, they do not kill for themselves until they are seven months old, and may stay with the parents for two years. They do not become mature until they are three. Although the cheetah is included in the cat family it differs in many ways from the typical cat. First, its claws are blunt and at best can be only partially retracted. Second, it is long-legged and depends on speed to capture its prey instead of hunting by stealth and final pounce.

Said to be the fastest land animal, the cheetah is credited with speeds of up to 70mph (112kph), but it cannot maintain this for long and its usual speed is 50mph (80kph) or less. There are usually three or four cubs in a litter (*below right*). Cheetah cubs can be recognized by their manes of straggling grey hair, their greyish backs, and their dark brown bellies. In their first weeks, the mother will haul straying cubs back to the nest by the scruff of the neck. By the age of two months the cubs have changed to adult coloring except that they still have a grey mane. Unlike the adult, the cheetah cub has sharp, retractile claws, and can climb trees well.

The civet (*top*) might be a tabby kitten, but for the prominent white patch either side of the nose. Yet civets, together with genets and mongooses, form a separate family from the cats (the Viverridae).

THE BEGINNINGS OF LIFE

The beginnings of life

With relatively few exceptions, every animal starts life as a fertilized egg-cell. The exceptions are the single-celled animals, and the few multicellular animals that reproduce by budding, fragmentation (that is, by pieces becoming detached from the parent body) or by the process which is known as parthenogenesis or 'virgin birth'.

Egg-laying animals

Most animals are oviparous. That is, the females lay eggs in which the fertilized ovum is surrounded by protective membranes, including an outer shell. In birds, this is hard and chalky. In reptiles, it is usually parchment-like. The ovum contains yolk granules to feed the growing embryo. In birds and reptiles, the yolk is a compact mass of food material. This larger quantity is necessary because the young are finally hatched in an advanced state of development, after a long period of incubation.

Live births

Mammals differ from all other animals in having a coating of hair on the body, and in suckling their young. All bear their young alive (a process known as viviparity), except for half-a-dozen species in Australasia, the echidnas or spiny anteaters, and the duckbill or platypus, which are collectively known as the egg-laying mammals.

Some reptiles and fishes produce their young by ovovivipary, a process halfway between oviparity and viviparity. In ovovivipary, the egg is retained in the body of the female, and hatches more or less at the moment of laying, giving the appearance of live birth.

Mammals are the most highly organized of all animals. As a consequence, their young require longer than most others to complete their development. But whereas birds' eggs are incubated by one or both parents, to keep the embryo warm, the mammal embryo stays within the mother's body. It receives food and oxygen through her blood, and protection and warmth from her body. The warmth is especiall important for the offspring of warmblooded animals.

The embryo

In the early stages of its life, any animal is no more than a group of cells, as we have seen. Even as it begins to take shape it still looks, to the uninformed eye, somewhat featureless. This is the embryo. Later, in all but the lowest animals, there comes a time when limbs begin to grow out from the body, and the head, with its eyes and mouth, is recognizable. In terms of strict dictionary definition, this is the foetus (often spelt fetus). In practice, the word 'foetus' is applied only to the later stages of the mammalian offspring. For birds, reptiles and fishes, the word 'embryo' is used up to the time of hatching.

Gestation

The period of development from conception to hatching of the egg, or to parturition (that is, giving birth) in mammals, is known as the gestation. Again, it is usual to speak of gestation only in the case of mammals. For birds, and for those animals in which one of the parents remains with the eggs until they hatch, this sam interval is usually spoken of as the period of incubation.

The length of time needed for incubation or gestation varies with the species, but is roughly linked with the size of the parents. The incubation period for the goldcrest, the smallest of British birds, is 14–17 days. That of the ostrich, the largest living bird, is around 40 days. Other large flightless birds related to the ostrich, such as the emu, have an incubation period nearer to 60 days.

The smallest living mammal is the Palestine pygmy shrew, 3.8cm (1.5 inches) long in head and body, and with a tail 2.5cm (1 inch) long (about the size of the goldcrested wren). It has a gestation of three weeks or slightly less. The African elephant, the male of which may weigh six tons, has a gestation of nearly two years. On the other hand, the blue whale, the largest animal that has ever lived, 30 metres (100 feet) long, has a gestation slightly less than one year. Even so, the exceptionally short gestation of the blue whale does not materially upset the general principle that the larger the mammal, the longer is the gestation, as a few selected examples show:

Gestation times

house mouse	20–21 days
rat	20–23 days
rabbit	28–33 days
cat, fox	52–63 days
wolf, dog, jackal, coyote	60–63 days
pig	111–120 days
sheep, goat	144–154 days
cow	276–289 days
horse	330–344 days
camel	390–400 days
giraffe	420–455 days

Precocious babies

A second factor affecting comparative figures of this kind is illustrated by the guinea pig. This is not much bigger than a common rat, yet its gestation period is 63–70 days, against 20–23 for a rat. The explanation is that baby rats are born at an earlier stage of development, blind, naked and helpless, they need to be suckled for three weeks and make little attempt to take solid food before then. In contrast the baby guinea-pig is markedly precocious. It is born with eyes open, fully-furred, and is able to run about soon after birth. It is not weaned for three weeks, but it begins to nibble solid food within twenty-four hours of birth.

Guinea-pigs, and others able to feed themselves soon after birth, are known as precocial young.

Altricial babies

Animals born helpless and needing to be tended and kept warm in a nest for a while after birth are called altricial, meaning that after hatching they have to be fed by parents. Precocial young require a longer gestation simply because they are born at a later stage of development than altricial young.

A further example of this difference is seen in the European rabbit and the hare. The two animals are of similar size, but one is altricial, the other precocial. Young rabbits are born blind, naked and helpless in a nest. The leverets (young hares) are born with eyes open, fully furred, and able to move about soon after birth. The gestation in the rabbit is 28–33 days; in the hare, 32–43 days.

Cells mark time

One of the more remarkable phenomena in the field of reproduction is what is known as delayed implantation. When the fertilized ovum has been dividing for a while, the mass of cells so formed is converted into a hollow sphere known as the 'blastocyst'. In mammals, the blastocyst becomes implanted into the wall of the uterus, where the cells continue to develop. In some species, the blastocyst fails to become implanted, and lies free in the uterus for a period of time. After a while it does become implanted, and further development proceeds as if there had been no time-gap.

WATER BABIES

Many different forms of life exist in water, or come to the water in search of food. Obviously fish spend their entire lives in the water. Other creatures, such as the seal, spend most of their lives in the water, but return to the land to give birth. By contrast, the frog (*left*) lives most of its life on land, but returns to the water to have its young.

For two thousand million years all plants and animals lived in water. Then, four hundred million years ago the first land plants appeared. This prepared the way for animals to invade the land.

Some animals, such as the land crabs, even today are able to live on land, but have to go back to water to lay their eggs. The same is usually true of amphibians like frogs and toads. The larvae of frogs and toads are called tadpoles. They are fish-like in shape at first, with a long tail. Later, when legs are grown, the tail is gradually absorbed. The froglet of the European frog (*previous page*) is almost ready to leave the water. Only a stump of a tail is left.

The larvae of the freshwater eel are peculiar in the very long journey they make. The parents leave the rivers of North America and Europe and travel across the Atlantic to the ocean depths near the Sargasso Sea. There they spawn. The larvae hatching from the eggs return to the rivers from which their parents came. Those going to America take a year for the journey. Those going to Europe take over two years. Arriving at the coast, the larvae change into elvers (*top left*), or baby eels, then swarm up the rivers in their millions to feed and grow. Eventually they return to the Sargasso Sea.

Salmon do the reverse. The adults feed in the sea but go up the rivers to spawn. The young salmon, alevins (*top right*), hatch carrying on their undersides a yolk sac filled with nutritious material which they absorb. Only when the yolk is exhausted do the young salmon need to search for food.

The midwife toad (*bottom left*) is peculiar in a different way. The male alone brings the babies into the world. The female lays her eggs in strings. The male entangles these around his legs and carries them about with him. He goes to water periodically and immerses them, to keep them from drying out. When the eggs are due to hatch, he makes a final visit to water to release the tadpoles into their natural element.

The African clawed frog is another oddity. It lives all the time in water, feeling for food with its sensitive toes, and using them to stuff it into its mouth. Its tadpole (*right*) is peculiar, too. On hatching it remains motionless at the surface for a week, unable to feed because it has no mouth. When its mouth does appear it does not nibble food, as other tadpoles do. It sucks in a variety of small single-celled animals living among the algae.

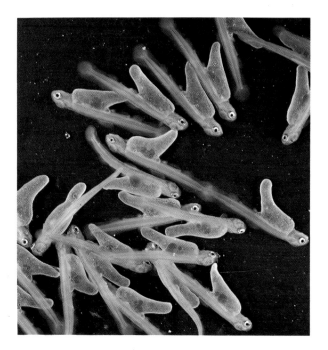

Sea mammals

Seals are carnivores, related to dogs, so their babies are called pups. By contrast, parent seals are known as bulls and cows. The baby harp seal (*below*), of the Arctic, has a white coat, but here it is tinged yellow with the birth, or amniotic, fluids.

Slightly more advanced is the baby South American fur seal (*bottom right*) from the coast of Argentina.

Seals are descended from land mammals and as such must come ashore to give birth. The exception to this rule are the whales, represented here by the southern white whale (*right*), of the Southern Seas. The baby whale enters the world by breech birth, that is tail-first, and the moment it is free of the mother must swim to the surface to take its first breath. The mother is watchful, and if necessary will help the baby to the surface with her muzzle.

Reptiles

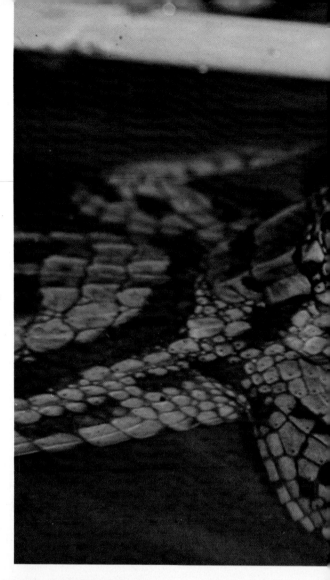

Turtles and crocodilians, which include
crocodiles, alligators, caimans and gharials,
are aquatic to the extent that they spend most
of their time in water. Yet they frequently come
out on land to bask. They are among the oldest
types of reptiles, having reached a peak for size
during the great Age of Reptiles, associated in
our minds with the dinosaurs. In their form and
anatomy they have changed little over the last
hundred million years. Their breeding habits
also appear to be unchanged, for although tied

to water both turtles and crocodilians must come on land to lay their eggs.

The leatherback or leathery turtle, the largest of the marine turtles, makes long journeys by sea to tropical coasts where the females drag themselves laboriously up the beach to dig pits in the sand in which to lay. The baby leatherback (*top left*) unerringly makes its way toward the sea.

Similarly, crocodilians, such as the Nile crocodile (*left*) and the American alligator (*top right*) lay their eggs in shallow pits, covering them with sand or rotting vegetation. It used to be thought the hatchlings found their own way to water, but it was discovered a few years ago that the mother, sometimes assisted by the father, takes hatchlings a few at a time in her mouth and carries them to water. She then washes them and releases them into the water.

BABY BIRDS

All birds lay eggs. They build nests
to keep the eggs together, and to ease
the task of guarding them. The parent
birds must keep the eggs close to
body temperature throughout their
development. Once the eggs are
hatched, some chicks emerge blind
and naked while others have a fine,
downy coat and soon leave the nest.

Flamingos (*previous page*) count as water birds in the sense that they feed in water and only come on land if disturbed. Even as babies they do not set foot on dry land. The nest is a circular mound of mud with a depression in the top to contain the eggs. It is made in water, in a lake or slow-flowing river in tropical or subtropical countries. The baby, hatched after four weeks' incubation, has short legs. It stays in the nest for two to three days, and after that can swim. Ten weeks later the young flamingo is able to fly and to feed itself.

Two extremes of birds are seen in the ostrich and the penguin, although both are flightless. The ostrich (*below*) is polygamous, the family group comprising of one male to three to five hens, sharing one nest of up to 50 or more eggs and a nursery of as many chicks. They live in desert conditions. King penguins (*right*), by contrast, are models of marital fidelity. They lay a single egg in a harsh environment but draw nourishment from the abundance of life in the sea. Their chicks also associate in groups, in a crêche, while the parents are away fishing.

Not all birds are active during the day. Some are nocturnal: they sleep during the daylight hours, and are active at night.

Owls, represented here by the spotted eagle owl chicks of Africa (*left*), are nocturnal birds of prey, feeding especially on warm-blooded prey.

The white or masked booby (*below*), of the Galapagos Islands, with its fledgeling, feeds by day by diving into the sea for fish.

The European white stork in its nest (*right*) feeds itself and its chicks by foraging, especially during the day, on any small food that moves on land or in water. The Stork nestlings are at first fed on frogs, small mammals and large insects brought up from the parent's crop in a slimy mass. Later, they gulp whole animals brought in and dropped in front of them.

THE SURVIVAL INSTINCT

Every baby animal is adapted to its environment as it develops. It must learn to fend for itself as soon as possible. Some animals need to spend a long time learning from its parents' example. Others, such as the mute swan cygnets (*left*), enter the world equipped with the ability to swim and to feed themselves. But the instinct to survive on the part of the young, and the instinct to preserve their own species, prompts some adult and baby animals to indulge in characteristic behavior patterns that are both effective and charming.

Some mammals habitually carry their babies from place to place, as the need arises, often carrying them in their mouths. This is mostly found in rodents and carnivores, the flesh-eating mammals. It is extraordinary that it should be so marked in flesh-eaters, for the mere presence between their teeth of a warm soft body should, by any reckoning, excite their instinct to bite.

Nevertheless, while transporting the very young – typically by holding the baby by the neck or head, although any other part of the body will do – the flesh-eating instincts are temporarily suppressed.

Equally interesting is the failure of the baby to object to this, especially since the touch of a stranger evokes at least a show of hostility, even in a tiger cub (*left*) or a baby leopard (*above*). The reason is that the cub has been accustomed to it before its eyes have opened.

A spiny mouse (*top left*), of Africa, demonstrates the more usual way in which rodent mothers transport their babies. They grasp the infant across its middle with their teeth so that it hangs spine downwards. This is the pattern when the mother is performing her task unhurriedly. In an emergency she may grasp the baby unceremoniously by any part that is near her mouth. Because rodent babies grow quickly and soon put on weight, transport by the parent is seldom possible once the babies' eyes are open. Since the babies soon learn to run, however, they can then follow the mother about, as in the family of golden hamsters (*below*).

Carrying young follows an entirely different pattern in the marsupials, the pouch bearing mammals of Australasia and America. The kangaroo is a good example.

The koala, (*right*) which lives in Australia, is also a marsupial. The early stages of the baby's life follow closely those of the baby kangaroo. When, however, the baby koala is too large to remain comfortably in the pouch, it rides on the mother's back. Koalas live in trees, which demands great skill in movement, and the young soon learn to be as efficient as their parents.

Nestlings

Nestlings which remain in the nest until they are ready to fly, display instinctive behaviour patterns that ensure that they are fed. When they feel hungry they open their bills wide, (*left*) exposing the bright lining inside. This bright color (often red or yellow) stimulates the parent bird to drop food into the gaping beaks of the young.

The nestlings for their part only gape when they sense or see the parent has come back to the nest. As soon as they sense that the parent is arriving, the nestlings peer up, stretch their necks vertically and open wide their mouths. Just as a human mother puts a spoonful of food into her infant's gaping mouth, so a parent bird fills the gaping beak of a nestling. In the bird it is wholly instinctive. It is also compulsive, as when the reed warbler (*above*) pushes food into a cuckoo's gaping throat. The hoopoe (*right*) demonstrates the same compulsion, but in this instance with its own young.

INDEX

Italicized numbers refer to
illustrations

FRONT COVER PHOTOGRAPH:
HANS REINHARD/BRUCE
COLEMAN LTD.
BACK COVER PHOTOGRAPH:
MITCH REARDON/TONY STONE
WORLDWIDE

This edition published in 1990 by
Treasure Press, Michelin House,
81 Fulham Road, London SW3 6RB

© 1979 Octopus Books Limited

ISBN 1 85051 490 9

Produced by Mandarin Offset
Printed in Hong Kong